To:

From:

IF THE *Shoe* FITS

Written and compiled by
Lois L. Kaufman and Rasheen Hewlett

Illustrated by Paula Brinkman

PETER PAUPER PRESS, INC.
WHITE PLAINS, NEW YORK

Illustrations copyright © 1998
Paula Brinkman

Designed by Arlene Greco

Text copyright © 1998
Peter Pauper Press, Inc.
202 Mamaroneck Avenue
White Plains, NY 10601
ISBN 0-88088-833-4
Printed in China
13 12 11 10 9 8 7

Visit us at www.peterpauper.com

IF THE *Shoe* FITS

INTRODUCTION

Every woman can see her own history reflected in her wardrobe of shoes—what she wore with the shoes, where she went, whom she was with. We strongly believe that a passion for shoes is indicative of a passion for life—and so we have collected this small treasure-trove of shoe lore and fact.

Give a girl the correct footwear and she can conquer the world, said Bette Midler. Perhaps that's what Imelda Marcos was looking for as she accumulated over 2,700 pairs of shoes. At any rate, it would be fun to try.

L. L. K. and R. H.

The average person takes 9,000 steps per day, and walks the equivalent of 3 $\frac{1}{2}$ times the circumference of the earth in a lifetime.

The first shoes were probably
made of woven grass or rawhide
tied to the feet by means of
thongs. We would likely describe
them today as sandals.

Evidence of shoemaking has been found dating back to 10,000 B.C.

Ancient wall paintings depict Egyptian sandal makers at work.

The average American
buys five pairs
of shoes per year.

Michael Jackson dances in loafers,
as did Gene Kelly.

Fred Astaire wore traditional dress
shoes for his movie dancing.

Vogue magazine did its first big article on shoes in 1919, featuring footwear for all occasions.

In the United States, it was common until the 1950s to X-ray feet in shoe stores with a fluoroscope.

In the 19th century,
the French had special shoes
made to crush walnuts.

Phil Knight, a reclusive
billionaire, expanded Nike
from a two-person importing
company into a $4 billion
worldwide business.

King Tut's tomb contained a pair
of jeweled sandals.

The first high-heeled shoe can be
traced to ancient Greece. It also
had a thick sole, and made the
wearer as much as 6 inches taller.

In ancient Egypt, sandals
indicated power and rank;
the underclass went barefoot.
Different social classes in
ancient Greece could also be
identified by their footwear.

Shoes play a critical role in
such fairy tales and heroic stories
as *Puss in Boots, Seven-League
Boots,* and *Cinderella.*

The Emperor Nero's wife,
Poppaea, reportedly had her
horses shod with gold shoes.

Napoleon Bonaparte's servants
broke his shoes in for him by
wearing them first.

Marie Antoinette had
a servant whose only job
was to take care of her shoes
(reportedly 500 pairs).

The foot contains one-fourth of
all the bones in the human body.

In the 15th century German
knights rode to battle in armor
shoes with pointed toes.

In ancient China, women's feet were bound in infancy to keep them tiny and thus more attractive.

There were 8 pairs of ruby
slippers made for Judy Garland
in her role as Dorothy in
The Wizard of Oz. The last pair
sold at auction for $165,000.

The Bass Weejun, introduced
in 1936, quickly became
a unisex fashion known to us
all as "loafers."

The wedge heel,
a standard today, was invented
by Italian shoe designer
Salvatore Ferragamo in 1936.

Until the end of the 18th century
in Europe, clogs made of wood,
or wood plus other materials,
were the footwear worn
by ordinary people.

Greta Garbo once bought
70 pairs of the same
style shoes—but in
different colors.

The slippers in the original
French story of Cinderella were
made of fur, not glass. The
change came in the translation
from French to English
(*vair*—fur, was taken
for *verre*—glass).

The boots worn by Neil
Armstrong on the moon in
1969 were left there to prevent
contamination when
he returned to earth.

In the United States,
parents often have their
baby's first shoes bronzed,
as a keepsake of his or
her babyhood.

Pointy-toed shoes became
popular around the 14th century,
and the fashion spread all
over Europe and beyond.
Sometimes the points were
so long that they had to be
tied up to keep them
from dragging.

In England, in 1363,
a law prescribed the length
of the pointed toe according
to class; the longest toe was
reserved for nobility.

It was a custom in China
to throw a bride's red shoe up
on the roof on the couple's
wedding night to insure
marital love and harmony.

Left-handed people are
also left-footed. In other words,
they tend to take the first step
with the left foot.

The high curved heel which
we call the Louis heel goes
back to Louis XIV of France
in the 17th century. He wore
them to appear taller.

In some religions,
shoes are offered as
sacrifices to gods.

In many cultures, shoes have had a strong association with religion and religious practices.

Muslims, Hindus, and Orthodox Jews remove their shoes before entering holy places.

The shoe had legal significance
to the ancient Hebrews,
who used it to seal a bargain.

There is evidence that ancient
people commissioned burial shoes
to be made as status symbols
for the next world.

Elton John's famous
platform-sole boots were
made specially for him,
and added a needed 6 inches
to his height.

"Earth Shoes," first marketed in
the U.S. in 1970, were made so
that the heel was lower than the
toes, and were supposed to
encourage better posture and
to be more comfortable.

Up to the middle of the 19th century, shoes were made with virtually the same hand tools used by the ancient Egyptians.

In the 16th century,
shoes called *chopines* had
platforms so high that they
were almost like stilts.

Mass production of shoes began
in the mid-19th century, and
helped produce one of the worst
forms of sweatshop labor.

The making of different shoes
for left and right feet did not
become a general practice
until the 19th century.

In American colonial days, a
shoemaker would live with a
family for the time required
to make all the shoes the
family needed. Then he
would move on.

The first known shoemaker
in America was Thomas Beard,
who came to Salem,
Massachusetts, in 1629.
The shoe industry developed
in New England from that start.

The McKay machine, invented in 1858, permitted production of low-cost shoes by eliminating hand-sewing.

St. Crispin is the patron saint of shoemakers.

The shoes tied to the bridal car are a remnant of the custom of the bride's parents giving her shoes to the groom as a sign of her leaving their house forever.

Tying shoes to a newly-wed couple's carriage or car was also meant as a fertility symbol.

Marlene Dietrich reportedly
wore each pair of her Ferragamo
shoes only once or twice before
buying new ones.

The word "sabotage" comes
from a period in history when
workmen protested job layoffs
by casting their wooden shoes,
called *sabots*, into the machinery
and thus stopping production.

Queen Victoria owned
black leather shoes with
glass monograms.

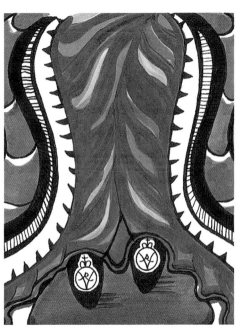

Abraham Lincoln was
known to shine his own boots
in the White House.

Our cave-dwelling ancestors
wrapped animal skins or
furs around their feet for
warmth and protection,
and shoes evolved
from that time.

In Europe, it was once
considered a good-luck charm
to place a shoe inside a wall
when building a house.

The world's largest shoe,
on display at the Scholl College
of Podiatric Medicine, is a size 35.
It belonged to Mr. Robert
Wadlow, of Alton, Illinois.
Later in his life, at full growth,
Mr. Wadlow towered at 8' 11.1"
and wore a size 44 shoe.

The word "moccasin,"
describing Algonquin Indian
soft-bottom footwear, originated
in northeastern North America
centuries ago. The general style
of moccasins is still
popular today.

The first people known to wear high heels for riding horses were Mongol tribesmen who wore bright wooden heels. They were nobles, and obviously had the money required to own and care for a horse. We still describe someone with wealth as being "well-heeled."

Every woman has an actual
physical need for shoes. . . .
If this craving cannot be satisfied,
women will and often do become
irrational and cannot be held
responsible for their actions.

MIMI POND,
Shoes Never Lie

SHOE SONGS

Blue Suede Shoes

Oh, Them Golden Slippers

Give Me That Old Soft Shoe

Shoe Fly Pie

These Boots Were Made
for Walking

Shoe Me the Way to Go Home

Rings on Her Fingers,
Bells on Her Toes

Shoe Be Do Be Do

Boots and Saddles

Mule Train

Tiptoe through the Tulips

Shoes with Wings on

O Sole Mio

BOOKS AND STORIES

The Worn-out Dancing Shoes
(Grimm fairy tale)

Cinderella

History of Little
Goody Two-Shoes

Mercury's Winged Sandals

The Leatherstocking Tales

Puss in Boots

The Shoes of the Fisherman,
by Morris L. West

The Old Woman in the Shoe

MOVIES AND SHOWS

The Red Shoes
(from an Andersen fairy tale)

The Man with One Red Shoe

High Button Shoes

A Yank at Oxford